IMAGES
of America

FORT MILES

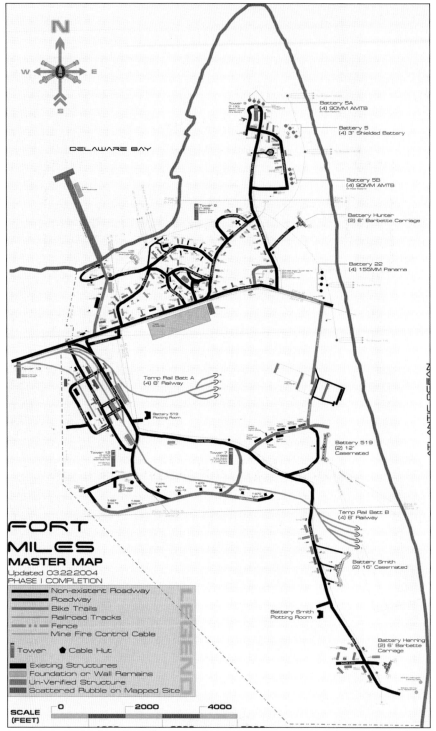

This recent drawing displays the full extent of armament on Cape Henlopen. From the northern point of the cape to Herring Point on the southern extremity, Fort Miles bristled with guns. More than 2,000 soldiers lived and worked in the support areas behind the gun batteries.

IMAGES
of America

FORT MILES

Dr. Gary Wray and Lee Jennings

ARCADIA
PUBLISHING

Published by Arcadia Publishing
Charleston SC, Chicago IL, Portsmouth NH, San Francisco CA

Printed in the United States of America

Library of Congress Catalog Card Number: 2005929795

For all general information contact Arcadia Publishing at:
Telephone 843-853-2070
Fax 843-853-0044
E-mail sales@arcadiapublishing.com
For customer service and orders:
Toll-Free 1-888-313-2665

Visit us on the Internet at www.arcadiapublishing.com

CONTENTS

ACKNOWLEDGMENTS

As a boy growing up in West Virginia, I always loved reading about history, particularly military history. When I wasn't playing sports, I spent every extra minute at the local library soaking up the writings of Napoleon, Rommel, and Patton. While writing my senior college thesis about West Virginia in World War I, I was surprised to learn that my paternal grandfather, Roy Wray Sr., saw much combat as a tough enlisted man in the U.S. Expeditionary Force on the western front. His son, my father, Roy Wray Jr., served in the Army Air Corps in World War II as an aerial engineer/gunner on a B-26 Marauder. The exploits of my two paternal forebears spurred my interest in World War II, and I have spent the last four decades reading, writing, and studying everything to do with the greatest war of the last century. I thank the two Roy Wrays for inspiring me, their grandson and son, in this work. Our country is stronger due to their efforts and the efforts of millions of other American men and women who have answered the call to defend our beloved country. It is men and women like these who built and served at Fort Miles during World War II. I dedicate my part of this book to their efforts to protect us during our country's first homeland security endeavors.

—Dr. Gary Wray

The writing of this book and the development of the Fort Miles Historic Area as a World War II museum are the result of the hard work and support of many. We are very grateful to Nate Davidson and Mike Rogers, whose thousands of hours of volunteer work at the fort have made it come alive. Breanne Preisen spent many hours scanning and re-scanning pictures and documents, as well as scheduling oral histories with Fort Miles veterans. The exhibits staff gave great assistance to us. Georgia Vaughan has assisted in numerous ways. We deeply appreciate the work of the Fort Miles Historical Association, whose members have been instrumental in preparing the site for restoration. The staff of Cape Henlopen State Park, where the fort was located, has given whole-hearted support to the effort despite their already full schedule. In my 13-year tenure at the Division of Parks and Recreation, I have enjoyed the support of our director, Charles Salkin, whose commitment to historic preservation is total. I have been privileged to work under the management of Jim O'Neill. Jim is a firm believer in public history programs that are "Educational, Engaging, Edgy, and Entertaining." His strong support, boundless sense of adventure, and patience with a known risk-taker such as myself provided the catalyst for innovation. Veterans of the Coast Artillery and their families have donated invaluable collections of photographs, uniforms, and personal papers. The United States Naval Surface Warfare Center in Dahlgren, Virginia, and the Naval History Center have provided us with guns and equipment for the museum. The Army History Center has provided us with weapons and fire control equipment. The New Castle County Seabees Reserve Unit gave a great deal of their time and effort helping us to install the guns. Finally I wish to express my appreciation to the Coast Defense Study Group, whose scholarship and interest have been invaluable.

—Lee Jennings

INTRODUCTION

Little Delaware is not known as a military bastion for the United States, but an accident of geography has made her strategically important to the security of our country. The state occupies the western side of the Delaware Bay, and in the history of the United States, whoever controls Delaware Bay controls the great city of Philadelphia and its environs. During the Revolutionary War, several forts were built to protect that city. Prominent among these was Fort Delaware on Pea Patch Island, almost in the middle of the Delaware River. This massive masonry edifice was built to prevent a hostile fleet approaching Philadelphia in pre–Civil War America. During the Civil War, due in no small measure to its island location, Fort Delaware assumed the additional role of housing Confederate POWs.

As naval weapons improved in both power and range, the defenses along the Delaware moved further away from the cities they were designed to protect. Fort Delaware provides an excellent example, constructed 40 miles south of Fort Mifflin, which stands at the southern edge of the city. As weapons innovations continued at sea, so it went on land. Smooth-bore cannons gave way to rifled guns; muzzle-loading guns gave way to breech loaders. The size, weight, and sophistication of ammunition available to gunners on both sides increased exponentially. The 350-year history of fortification on the Delaware may be viewed abstractly in this way. During the Revolutionary War, American soldiers watched British cannonballs fall and roll. When they stopped rolling, they were handed over to American gunners to fire back at the foe. The last fort on the Delaware, Fort Miles fired shells weighing more than 2,000 pounds at targets their gunners could not even see. Catching one to shoot back was, of course, out of the question.

At the beginning of the 20th century, harbor defenses across the country were modernized. Fort Delaware received 37-ton breech-loading 12-inch guns mounted on carriages that allowed them to disappear from view after they were fired. The defense site on Pea Patch Island was joined by two others, Fort Mott in New Jersey and Fort DuPont on the Delaware side. These forts housed weapons of at least eight different calibers. The guns and carriages were still experimental. Testing at Fort DuPont resulted in an 8-inch carriage flying apart when the gun was fired. Fire control systems were still being developed, as evidenced by newspaper reports of shells fired from Fort DuPont landing in nearby Salem, New Jersey, resulting in the destruction of a hay wagon and the expressed desire of the town that the army attempt to aim more carefully in the future. Continued improvement to artillery moved into the ballistic range. Guns on ships and ashore aimed to fire in high arcs, resulting in plunging fire, rendering the early-20th-century forts obsolete. In 1917, the harbor defenses moved south yet again to Fort Saulsbury. The 12-inch guns situated along the Murderkill River could reach the mouth of the bay; however, they were out in the open without cover from aircraft.

The years between the world wars saw little actual improvement to harbor defenses. Planners began to understand the impact that aircraft could make. Designs were drawn to place the guns in steel-reinforced concrete casemates and to limit the weapons types to 16-inch and 6-inch, a match for anything then afloat. Lewes, Delaware, was to be the site of one these modern defenses.

The Great Depression and the lack of threat postponed any development until the very last minute. In 1940, with the growing threat of war, the government began to fortify the mouth of the bay. Delaware's own National Guard unit, the 261st Coast Artillery, was federalized and moved to the beach from its location in the western part of Sussex County. It was this unit, made up of Delaware men, who were tasked with building the place they were to call Camp Henlopen. They were soon joined by the 21st Coast Artillery, then training in mine warfare at Fort DuPont.

The day after Pearl Harbor was attacked, Col. George Ruhlen, commander of the harbor defense of the Delaware, then headquartered at Fort DuPont, received the message from high command to "set Condition Two immediately." Placing his existing assets at full war alert was easier said than done. The harbor defenses in place consisted of a number of 155-mm towed artillery pieces that could certainly not stand up to battleships. The 21st Coast Artillery energetically began to plant an extensive controlled minefield across the bay. Old three-inch guns from Fort Delaware and the New York sector provided rapid-fire defense coverage over the minefield as well as a semblance of anti-air capability. Very poor phone and radio communication between command in Delaware City and Fort Miles on the ocean greatly complicated the task set for the troops. Command was soon passed to the new fort.

Fort Miles as originally conceived was to boast two dual batteries of 16-inch guns and two of 6-inch guns. Upon America entering the war, however, most of the major German surface assets were out of action, sunk, or heavily damaged. The decreasing threat resulted in changes to the plan. Two 12-inch guns moved from Fort Saulsbury took the place of two of the 16-inch guns. Modern 90-mm weapons took over air defense. Nineteenth-century railroad guns were removed as more modern types came on line. The war was finished before the fort was. What *was* finished was obsolete.

During the war, the fort became one of most formidable and, at $24 million, one of the most expensive in the U.S. coastal inventory. Fort Miles was designed to fight the strongest elements of the German surface fleet, including the huge 15-inch guns of the battleships *Bismarck* and *Tirpitz*. While it was never the intent of the Nazi planners to send those ships against the American coast, our planners could not be certain, compelling them to assume the worst case. If those major elements of the German surface fleet appeared off the coast and encountered the fort, it would have been an interesting and intriguing combat.

Delaware is fortunate to have not one but two of the greatest forts in the U.S. inventory in Fort Miles and Fort Delaware. The state of Delaware recognizes these assets and has placed a high priority on the restoration, preservation, and interpretation of these sites. It has been an effort assisted by many Delaware citizen-volunteers, including the Fort Miles Historical Association. Veterans of the 261st and 21st Coast Artillery add their stories and photograph collections to support efforts to tell the story of Fort Miles during the Second World War.

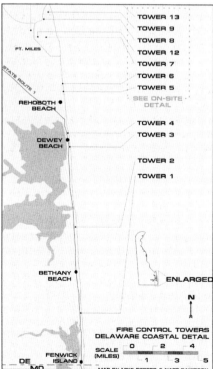

The most visible artifacts of World War II fortifications on the Delaware Bay are the 11 fire control towers lining the beach from Lewes to Bethany. The tall gray cylindrical towers have long been the source of curiosity and folk lore. These towers were in fact the "eyes of the guns," containing the instruments used to determine range and speed of incoming targets. The concrete used in construction of these towers made use of abundant beach sand. They were intended to last no more than 10 years. Today Tower 7 is open to the public for programs and tours.

One

SAND TO SUPER FORT
Camp Henlopen to Fort Miles

Lewes, the land destined to hold one of the largest seacoast fortifications in the United States, boasts a long and distinguished history. The site of the first European settlement in Delaware was nearby. Battles raged in the bay during the Revolutionary War and the War of 1812. It would appear that William Penn wished to preserve this area as open space for the benefit of all. Various governmental agencies occupied space on this land. A quarantine station that screened immigrants for contagious disease was located here. The U.S. Life-Saving Service and its successor, the U.S. Coast Guard, maintained stations here. During the First World War, the army set up experimental gun platforms in the area. In 1938, the 52nd Coast Artillery brought railroad guns into Lewes. Local citizens helped build temporary rail lines into what would become Fort Miles. The 52nd conducted target practice during the summer, firing at towed targets day and night—sight and sounds that are still fresh in the minds of those who observed them.

By 1940, a fence surrounded the site and guards patrolled the perimeters. Inside, construction was underway. Troops began arriving early in 1941, setting up temporary tent quarters at the beach. Windswept sand, extreme heat and cold, biting flies, and the odor emanating from a nearby fish-processing plant conspired to make life uncomfortable at best. The 261st Coast Artillery manned the 155-mm guns along the shore. One gun was always manned and ready. The 21st Coast Artillery set up shop deploying mines. Fresh from their recent training at Fort Hancock in New Jersey, they proudly displayed the red "E for excellence" badge on their uniforms. Thirty-five groups of 13 mines each were planted in the ocean and bay. The officers and men of Fort Miles were beginning to settle in to the realities of war.

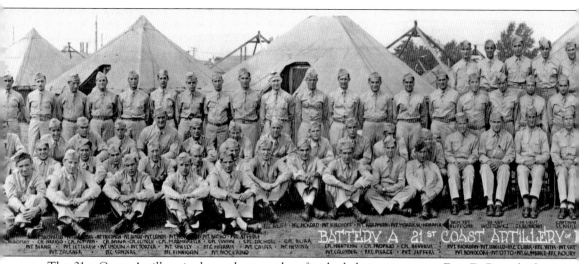

The 21st Coast Artillery is shown here as they finished their training at Fort DuPont, built quickly around an extant headquarters company. These men were trained in mine warfare and

DUPONT DEIL AT FORT HANCOCK N.J. AUGUST 23, 1941

anti-aircraft gunnery, jobs they assumed on arrival at Fort Miles.

Col. George Ruhlen was commander of harbor defenses of the Delaware at the onset of the war. Having received a number of war warnings, he was not surprised to receive the terse order to "set Condition Two immediately" on December 8, 1941. His headquarters were located at Fort DuPont in Delaware City, more than 60 miles from Camp Henlopen, which was lightly defended with 155-mm guns. Additional guns and ammunition were sent to satisfy Condition Two, which called for round-the-clock alerts for at least one gun. Ruhlen was relieved of command and replaced by Col. Robert Phillips on April 21, 1942. Headquarters, Harbor Defense of the Delaware, formally transferred to Fort Miles on June 7, 1942.

The oozlefinch, mascot of the coast artillery, is a "mythological fowl that only flies backwards, protecting its protuberant eyes from dust, and trivia." It is usually seen with its Latin motto *quid ad sceleratorum curamus*, roughly translated as "what the hell do we care?" The bird in this photograph belonged to Col. Riley McGarraugh, the last commander of Fort Miles.

Members of the 261st National Guard Company are shown at their training site in Georgetown, Delaware. In 1940, the 261st was federalized and sent to Fort Miles. Here a range communication section tests equipment.

The gun section of the 261st becomes familiar with the functions of a 155-mm "GPF" gun. These guns would become the first line of defense of the Delaware capes.

As headquarters of the harbor defenses of the Delaware prior to the war, Fort DuPont provided facilities for training of coast artillery troops and the Delaware National Guard. Members of the 21st Coast Artillery are seen here running through the extensive obstacle course in the marsh along the Chesapeake and Delaware Canal.

The range section masters the functions of plotting-room equipment. Plotters gathered information from observers. After collating the visual information with many complex variables, the range section then relayed information to the gunners for proper alignment of their guns and coordination of fire.

The communications section receives instruction in the use of radio transmitters. These complicated devices did not possess long-range capability.

Telephones of this type connected the gunners, observers, and plotters. Careful protocol was taught to each soldier to insure crisp communication.

In 1938, the 52nd Coast Artillery set up shop on the empty beach near Lewes. This is the spot that would later become Fort Miles. Notice the lack of vegetation and the handful of buildings in view. The 52nd normally trained at Fort Hancock in Sand Hook, New Jersey. This training tested the ability of the company to move its equipment quickly to a distant location. All aspects of organization were examined, from logistics to fire control.

The 52nd arrives with their railway guns for a spring drill. The train carried two 8-inch guns and two 8-inch mortars along with ammunition and range section cars. Local Lewes residents helped to build tracks into the site. They received a government commendation for their rapid and enthusiastic assistance.

This image clearly shows the eight-inch mortars carried by the 52nd. These high-trajectory but relatively short-range weapons began to fall out of favor with the coast artillery at the beginning of World War II.

Members of the 52nd prepare to set up their guns, which required long outriggers to stabilize the car during firing. An 8-inch mortar is seen here on its flatcar with an ammunition car and range-finding equipment. The guns were manufactured in the late 1890s but were still considered to be very accurate. Mortars were phased out of the coast artillery inventory in the beginning of World War II due in no small measure to their short range.

An 8-inch gun fires a round at a towed target offshore. The 1938 practice went very well indeed, with the exception of a night-fired round that came a bit too close to the tug pulling the target. Guns of this type were actually obsolete by 1942. They did provide an effective stop-gap until more modern batteries could be completed. Residents of the area who witnessed the practice were reassured by their return at the onset of the war. As a matter of pure speculation, it is interesting to consider the result of a modern German fleet attack against these rather ancient weapons.

An 8-inch mortar is reloaded. The shells weighed in at over 300 pounds, requiring a hoist to bring them into position. With hard work and practice, the crew could fire two rounds in 60 seconds. Although the picture says the mortar is 12 inches, only 8-inch mortars were used.

These are examples of the artwork of the coast artillery. Eight-inch shells are decorated with chalk markings. Girlfriends' names were popular ornaments. After the prewar years, the shells were addressed colorfully to the foe.

The gun section of the 52nd departs for Fort Hancock in 1938. They would return in two years' time under very different circumstances.

Col. Robert E. Phillips was the first commander at Camp Henlopen.

This was a temporary building at Camp Henlopen. The mess hall is set for a Christmas dinner. For many of the boys, this was their first Christmas away from home. As it turned out, it would not be the last. Menus for the dinner included: clam cocktail, turkey rice soup, oysterettes, roast tom turkey, snowflake potatoes, Virginia boiled ham, plum pudding with sauce, mince pie, grape punch, sweet cider, cigars, and after-dinner mints.

Here is a glimpse of the sparse conditions at Camp Henlopen. Overhead communications wire can be seen in this shot. Officers and enlisted men shared living conditions until improvements were made.

This is a tent city at Camp Henlopen. Pyramid tents with added wooden sides helped to reduce the cold somewhat. Coal heaters in the tents helped keep the occupants warm during the worst months. Cold-water showers were all that were available.

This guard shack was put up as the camp became a fort. A fence surrounded the property, which was constantly patrolled. Local residents were hired as watchmen until the outbreak of war, when the military police took over.

The main gate with the barrier in place shows the fence topped with barbed wire and the concrete posts that held the gate in place. These posts can still be seen at what is now the entrance to Cape Henlopen State Park.

This is a view down the main company street as seen by 261st member William Smith. Notice the plank walkways and the increase in order from the previous pictures.

This is a temporary latrine in the cantonment area. Note the lack of walkways both here and in the other cantonment areas. In rainy weather, ankle-deep mud added to the challenges of living at the beach.

Fort Miles, Delaware, 1941. Battery C, 261st CA (HD). Latrine for Battery C. Photo courtesy William A. Smith.

Pvt. Horace Knowles appears outside his tent in his dress uniform. Horace, a CCC employee prior to the war, contributed construction expertise during the Camp Henlopen period. Knowles assisted in the construction of wooden outer walls around the tents, providing an extra barrier to the cold wind and sand.

Knowles (right) and a friend relax, awaiting a possible call to duty. Knowles worked in a number of places, but during the early war, he helped man the 155-mm guns on the beach.

Here the 155-mm guns are shown in action at the cape. The crew prepares to load another round in practice. Note that they all carry gas masks in shoulder bags. Also note the World War I–type helmets. National Guard units were slow to receive newer equipment.

The 155-mm rounds were carried to the guns by two men who cradled the shells in leather carry straps.

Searchlights such as this one illuminated the night skies and waters to help gunners locate targets before the advent of radar. These lights carried their own electrical generators. Sixty-inch lights could throw a beam far out into the bay or up into the air. These lights were manned at a level of readiness similar to that of the guns.

Fort Miles, Delaware, 1941. 261st CA (HD). The buglers station. Photo courtesy William A. Smith..

The bugler sounds his calls through this makeshift public address system. In later times, the bugle call to alert stations was enhanced by a pair of old French guns on the parade ground.

Fort Miles, Delaware, 1941. Captain (Chaplain) James H. Bishop. Photo courtesy William A. Smith.

The army saw to the spiritual life of the men. Here we see the chaplain examine a bulletin board showing the time and place of services. These services were always well attended.

rt Miles, Delaware, 1941. 261st CA (HD) Meterology (weather
ction. Photo courtesy William A. Smith.

The weather was of critical importance to the coast artillery. Wind speed and direction, barometric pressure, and humidity were all parts of the calculus determining where a shell would go when it was fired.

The headquarters company of the 21st rose quickly from a token force to full strength due to the efforts of men like Pvt. Wesley Banse, seen here in his office. A master of organization, Banse managed to keep every order, every pass, every newsletter, in short *everything* the army gave him.

Rudimentary telephone communication was installed early at Camp Henlopen. This portable telephone exchange could be set up fairly quickly to manage a battle or to facilitate internal communication.

Lt. Col. Henry K. Roscoe strikes a pose outside of his tent in winter dress. Note the wooden sidewalls of the tent. Enlisted men, including Horace Knowles, helped to build these wind breakers that made the tents far more comfortable.

Fort Miles, Delaware, 1941. LTC Henry K. Roscoe, Commander, 261st CA (HD) (Sep). Photo courtesy William A. Smith.

The army, ever mindful of morale, built this temporary and rather sparse post exchange. It was later replaced by a modern commissary.

attery Motor Pool Inspection, 261st Coast Artillery, Camp Henlop
te 1941. U. S. Army photo, courtesy Department of Military Affa
tate of Delaware.

As the photograph caption indicates, these vehicles stand ready for inspection. Heavy trucks were required to move ammunition and supplies in large quantities.

The 21st celebrates mass outside in good weather prior to the construction of the chapel.

The 52nd returned to Camp Henlopen at the outbreak of war. This time, however, it was not a drill. This photo shows a rail gun emplacement fully camouflaged with crossed sections of snow fence. This scheme was tested by firing the guns with super charges. Little damage resulted and the army was well pleased with the result.

Here, Camp Henlopen cooks prepare fresh bread for the troops. Hot meals helped ease the discomfort of living in tents on the beach. Veterans relate that lamb and chicken were frequent entrees. As on most posts, bakeries delivered bread and pastries to officers' quarters once they were established.

Prior to the construction of regular chow halls, the troops took their meals in tents or in the open as seen in this shot from the earlier visit of the 52nd to Lewes. Conditions and equipment had not changed during the brief lull.

Mess Hall, 261st Coast Artillery, Camp Henlopen, Fall of 1941. U. S Army photo, courtesy, Department of Military Affairs, State of Delaware.

One of the first buildings to go up at Camp Henlopen was this mess hall. A shortage of lumber in 1942 was a factor in the selection of cement block as the primary construction material for barracks and support buildings after that time.

Two

DEFENDING THE DELAWARE
1943–1945

The change from Camp Henlopen to Fort Miles had no measurable impact on the troops assigned to protect the harbor beyond getting them out of the tents and into dry buildings. Drills, alerts, 10-mile runs, and stints of guard duty remained the same. In the summer, the fish-packing plant continued to smell. However, the surroundings were changing very quickly. New barracks buildings were a welcome relief. Running water that was at least occasionally warm improved morale. Veterans the authors have spoken to always insist that the food was both plentiful and good.

As war seemed to move farther away from the shore, Fort Miles became an active town of about 2,500 souls. Soldiers and civilian employees pitched in, too, with sales of war bonds. Blood drives were a popular way to show support for the troops. Young men with time on their hands turned to other endeavors, as will be seen in this chapter. The fort was justifiably proud of its basketball and baseball teams. The football team at Fort DuPont, however, was the champion. In addition to sports, the Fort Miles Players presented a number of musical comedies as well as spoofs of the various goings-on around the post. The USO-sponsored dances featured some nationally known big bands as well as some celebrity visits for the troops. The local Red Cross girls were another popular addition.

Further enhancing the sense of community were the various newsletters generated from the headquarters company. *Coastal Bursts* always featured a coast artillery theme on its front cover. While military matters were rarely discussed in its highly censored pages, social matters were vividly portrayed. Marriages and engagements, transfers, and vacations home were all grist for the mill. Classic blunders and sly innuendo concerning infamous events elicited enthusiastic coverage.

This unusual community continued to build in size and complexity until war's end. When peace came, the change was instant and dramatic. It took fewer years to classify this important military complex as unnecessary than it took to build it.

Distinctive Insignia worn by members of the 261st Coast Artillery Battalion (Harbor Defense)(Separate)

The griffon-topped shield of the 261st Coast Artillery was worn as a shoulder patch. Notice the reference to the "Separate Coast Artillery."

FERITE FORTITER

This is the crest of the 21st Coast Artillery. The history of the 21st reflects a number of efforts to achieve a distinctive coat of arms. A number of different mottoes were offered. As with most things military at the time, the work had to be approved by different individuals who were widely scattered. Making the rounds of approval by mail could take months.

CLASS G unp.No. 38587

Copyright Office
Of the United States of America
THE LIBRARY OF CONGRESS
★ ★ ★ WASHINGTON ★ ★ ★

Certificate of Copyright Registration

This is to certify, in conformity with section 55 of the Act to Amend and Consolidate the Acts respecting Copyright, approved March 4, 1909, as amended by the Act approved March 2, 1913, that a photograph or other identifying reproduction of the

design for a work of art

named herein has been deposited in this Office, under the provision of the Act of 1909, and that registration of a claim to copyright for the first term of twenty-eight years has been duly made in the name of Commanding Officer, 21st. Coast Artillery, U.S.Army,

Fort Du Pont, Delaware.

Title: Coat of Arms, 21st. Coast Artillery, U.S. Army.
Per fess wavy or and gules a fret countercharged. Motto:
Ferite Fortiter. By George Ruhlen, of United States.

Copy received _____ Aug. 13,1941

Entry: Class G., unp., No. 38587

[SEAL]

C.D.Bowie
Register of Copyrights.

Here is the copyright for the coat of arms of the 21st Coast Artillery of the U.S. Army. The shield is divided into a top half of gold and a bottom half of red by a wavy line. A fret fills the shield, red against the gold background and gold against the red background. The unit's motto, *ferite fortiter*, is Latin for "bravely wild."

Fort Miles, Delaware, 1941. Members of the 261st CA (HD).

FORMER COMMANDING OFFICERS

LT. COLONEL A. L. HAGGART
(7 September 1943 - 1 March 1944)

Note the winter uniforms in this morning formation outside the barracks for the 261st. The temporary barracks shown would soon be replaced by concrete-block buildings.

Lt. Col. A. L. Haggert assumed command of the 21st on September 7, 1943. The company was involved fully in laying the mine field and setting up headquarters.

COLONEL GEORGE RUHLEN
(4 November 1940 - 16 April 1942)

COLONEL ROBERT E. PHILLIPS
(6 May 1942 - 18 May 1942)

COLONEL CHARLES H. BERLE
(16 April 1942 - 6 May 1942
18 May 1942 - 27 January 1943
27 May 1943 - 7 September 1943)

COLONEL HERBERT V. RYAN
(27 January 1943 - 27 May 1943)

Col. George Ruhlen, Col. Robert Phillips, Col. Charles Berle, and Col. Herbert Ryan, the commanding officers of the 21st, are shown in this quickly assembled history of the 21st.

Colors at Review, 17 June 1943, Fort Miles, Delaware.
(First Sergeant John W. Jones, Battery "C", 21st Coast Artillery
awarded American Spirit of Honor Medal)

Colors are on review here at the parade ground in front of the military police office and the post brig. Sgt. John Jones was awarded a medal for bravery while planting mines in the bay. He prevented injury to others by quickly reacting to a snapped cable.

U.S. Mine Planter (USMP) *Sylvester* is shown at sea. This ship, along with USMP *Frank*, planted hundreds of mines across the shipping channels into the Delaware. It was difficult and dangerous work. The mines were organized into 35 groups of 13 each. Laying the mines required the complex organization of plotting teams ashore and a small flotilla of sea craft working with extreme precision. On the bow of the planter, just above the name of the ship, the reader may observe the reel of 50-pair armored mine cable.

This yawl boat worked with the mine planters and the distribution boats. The yawl brought the heavy mine-connecting cables into shore.

This buoyant mine with an anchor was the first type of mine planted in the harbor. A modest charge of 500 pounds of TNT was housed in the spherical case. The anchor rested on the bottom, and a line paid out to set the mine at its desired depth. Twisting of the cables clockwise and counter-clockwise during changing tides caused damage to the connecting cables. The cables eventually snapped, allowing the inert mine to drift away. Needless to say, many who came upon the drifting mines were terrified by the sight. The solution was simple but expensive. The entire minefield was removed and replaced with M4 mines.

The floating mines were replaced by M4 ground mines. The M4 was six feet high and six feet in diameter at the base with a conical top. It had service hatches on the top and side which had cover plates about 18 inches in diameter. The top hole was used to mount the interior items, including a magnetic coil and the grounding straps. Three thousand pounds of granulated TNT were loaded into the top hatch as well. The granulated explosive looked somewhat like corn flakes and was loaded into the mine with brass scoops. The side hatch was used to mount the exploder mechanism and provided the entrance for the control cable. A thousand pounds of lead kept the mine in place on the bottom. The mines were painted olive drab with black identification numbers. All mines were pressure-tested and had to hold their seal for 24 hours without losing pressure before they were placed in storage. The mine in this photograph is being prepared for loading.

The mine field was organized into 35 groups of 13 mines each in lines across the bay from the breakwater to Hen and Chicken Shoals, the main shipping channel. The mines were electrically controlled and laid out in a surveyed grid. Mine defense can best be described as a game of Battleship. For example, the mine is detonated when the ship is at location C-8 on a horizontal and vertical grid. In this photograph, coast artillery troops practice with the M1910A1 azimuth instrument, used to determine the location of a target. Note that they are located in a fire control tower, looking out through one of the horizontal slits. They are connected by telephone to the mine control plotting room, where the fire control information is collated along with the electric triggers for the mines.

A cargo net is arranged on the mine dock in preparation for loading heavy equipment. Fred Ruleman (left) and a friend untangle knots in the netting. It is attached to a crane, creating a cradle for cargo.

This hydrophone is ready for loading on a ship. In addition to the mines planted by the army, the navy maintained at least four of the underwater microphones at the entrance to the bay. Their primary mission was to detect submarines attempting to enter the minefield.

A sailor examines the chart from a fluxometer. A submerged magnet loop attached to this unit detected large metal objects passing over it. This was yet another defense against submarines.

Fred Ruleman (right) and friend prepare to board a distribution boat. Distribution boats prepared the cable and distribution boxes for attachment to the mines. This was a difficult job in rough weather. The cable had to be spliced into a type of switch box that was attached to the main shore cable and then attached to the mine.

Coastal Bursts was a newspaper that performed much the same service that small local newspapers supply today. The cover of this edition shows a Halloween motif, featuring a witch carrying a buoyant mine under her broom.

The covers of these newsletters were drawn by a number of army artists. Second from right in this group is Cpl. Howard Schroeder, the creator of the witch and mine mentioned above. Schroeder went on to become one Delaware's most important artists.

Another version of the newspaper was written specifically for the 21st. Note the "censored" mark across the bottom. All mail and all internal publications were submitted to war department censors prior to final release.

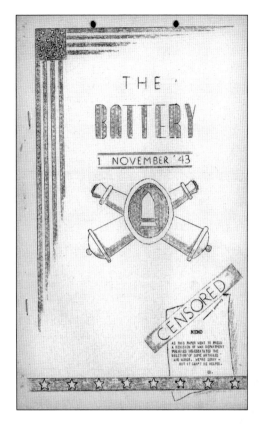

Christmas arrives at the beach in this clever send-up of Santa Claus in 1943. Christmas was a festive time on post. Mess halls were festooned with decorations, and lavish meals were the order of the day. Married soldiers were usually granted leave to spend the holidays at home.

Another look at Christmas 1943 is from the gun sections. Note the gun smoke creating the message "Merry Christmas."

This is the dedication ceremony for the new chapel in the summer of 1942. The block building with the white cross can be seen in the rear. The building currently serves as one of the summer youth camp buildings at Cape Henlopen State Park.

The basketball team of the 21st was a force to be reckoned with on the court. Teams from other service areas and some school teams provided the opposition. The football team at Fort DuPont was popular state wide, drawing thousands to its games against other posts and even local college teams. Sporting events of this type provided a much-needed source of entertainment for not only the military personnel but also for the surrounding communities.

Troops stand to sing the national anthem prior to a boxing match held at the post gym.

Fund-raising drives for many patriotic causes resulted in awards ceremonies such as the one featured here at Fort Miles.

THE "PAYOFF" AT FORT MILES: Three Second Service Command employees at Fort Miles, Delaware proudly display the. checks they received as awards in the War Department Suggestion Program. Pictured above (left to right) are: Mrs. Mae Godshall, Civilian Personnel Assistant; Colonel Robert E. Phillips, Commanding Officer of the Harbor Defenses of the Delaware; Kathryn D. Lingo; WOJG Carlton F. Scott, Post Personnel Officer; Harold W. Brummond and Charles Bell. Miss Lingo, Brummond and Bell were the award winners.

Public Relations Office   1/825   TDC/kp
Fort Miles, Delaware   FOR IMMEDIATE RELEASE:
     Lewes-2831

Fort Miles, Del., Feb. 20.

The War Department quickly rewarded those who made outstanding suggestions that resulted in a more efficient operation—especially ones that saved money. Despite an outward appearance of profligate spending, the army watched pennies carefully.

Safety was a vital concern to the commander of the post. In this photograph, the cake is inscribed with the words, "Fort Miles Safety Comm. 6 years perfect record. 898,024 man hours." This refers to the length of time without accidents. Where hundreds of tons of high explosives are kept, such a record is very desirable.

Talent abounded in areas other than the playing field and the plotting room. Here a budding group of thespians prepares and rehearses a musical comedy gently spoofing the commanding officer.

It's show time! The Fort Miles Players present *Here We Go*, a variety show featuring the Harbor Defense Band under the direction of Warrant Officer H. K. Schmidt. The opening number was, of course, the popular "Harbor Defense of the Delaware March." Proceeds from the show benefitted the State of Delaware Red Cross Camp and Hospital Council. The group was responsible for arranging "moving picture shows," equipping day rooms, and providing athletic equipment to the troops.

It is rehearsal night at the post theatre. With plenty of off-duty time and nowhere to go, involvement in shows at the fort was very popular.

The lack of women on the base did not deter our boys, as they were quick to jump into skirts and wigs for a show. From left to right are Pfc. Craig Edwards, Pvt. Paul Hillman, and Cpl. Charlie Lewis.

Soldiers take the stage at Fort Miles. A variety of plays and concerts took place on the post. On stage, these men run through a number called "My Sergeant and I Are Buddies."

Off-base assignments for the 261st included a short stint manning a 3-inch gun at the Liston Range Light in Bay View, Delaware, not far from Fort DuPont. The Triple Link Club was not far and provided ample entertainment.

Two officers of Battery C, 261st Coast Artillery Battalion (Harbor Defense)(Separate) on the steps of the clubhouse of the International Order of Odd Fellows on the property of the Bay View Improvement Company, Bay View, Delaware, spring 1942. This clubhouse and some surrounding property was leased by the Army to support the 3" Barbette mounted guns on the Coast Guard's Liston Range Front Lighthouse property. The clubhouse was used as the section's headquarters, mess hall and day room. The officer on the right is believed to be Lt. Howell. Photo courtesy William A. Smith.

Classes were offered and were mandatory for some. Lower ranks could attain higher-paying specialty jobs or higher rank by attending. Officers frequently reviewed the tactical situation, continuing to evolve their plans in the face of an ever-changing threat level.

unday afternoon visit by "Red Cross Girls" from Wilmington, Delawar
oring of 1942, at the Triple Link Clubhouse, Bay View Beach, Delawar
ased by the Army from the Bay View Improvement Company. Sergea
'illiam Smith is standing in the middle behind the card players. Pho
ourtesy William A. Smith.

Red Cross girls were a welcome addition to life on the post. Beyond delivering packages of toiletries and chocolate to the men, they helped to facilitate mail from home and sometimes furloughs for important family matters.

Blood Clinic Yields 600 Pints For Red Cross Unit at Fort Miles

Lewes-Rehoboth Volunteer Workers Help Mobile Group
Take Offerings From Civilians and Soldiers;
Millsboro Woman Served as Recorder

LEWES, Del., April 10—(Special).—More than 600 soldiers and civilians have just completed donations of a pint of blood at Fort Miles, through the Delaware chapter of the American Red Cross, which brought a mobile blood donor unit to the post for a three-day period.

This visiting unit from Baltimore previously received nearly 400 pints in a two-day stay at the Coast Artillery post in March.

A number of Red Cross volunteer workers from Lewes and Rehoboth Beach assisted the members of the blood donor unit. They included Mrs. Theodore D. Dick, Mrs. Jack Smock, Mrs. Jack Saff, Mrs. Barton Wallas, Miss Betty Ann Sullivan, Mrs. Betty Steele, Mrs. Edward Graham, Mrs. Alice Wilhelm, Mrs. Ralph Morgan, and Miss Alice B. Conner, all of Rehoboth Beach.

Lewes assistants who volunteered their services were Mrs. G. Clifton Maull, Mrs. Lyons Richardson, Mrs. Herman Short, Mrs. Sanford Clifton, Mrs. Kenneth Givan, Mrs. Mervyn Lafferty, Mrs. Raymond R. Atkins, Mrs. J. Wright Rowland,

Mrs. John E. McGovern and Mrs. Vivian Nelson.

Mrs. J. Reese White of Millsboro, chairman of the Sussex County Camp and Hospital Council, served as recorder. Miss Elizabeth Straughn, chairman of the Delaware Blood Donor Committee, and Robert C. Heaney, Red Cross field director at Fort Miles, made the arrangements for the blood donations with Captain Marc J. Matsen, special service officer, and Lieut.-Col. Frederic A. Hall of Public Relations.

Blood drives showed support for the troops and the cause. These events were always well attended by soldiers and civilian workers on the base and by the local residents.

The Fort Miles Orchestra prepares to strike up a tune for an Officers' Club party. It is interesting to note that each company of coast artillery had its own band or bands. Movement orders sent batteries out to different assignments either "less band" or "with band."

This Valentine's Day dance at Fort Miles was packed. Many of the men of the 261st were local and had wives or sweethearts near by. Others met local girls at frequent dances on the post.

Soldiers gather to watch a show at the post theatre. Popular movies were shown regularly at the fort theater for a nominal fee.

A change in the minefield brought a change of decoration to the fort. Here a soldier leans on an empty mine case marking the entrance to his building. After the buoyant mines were brought in, many were used in this manner throughout the post.

Three

THE GUNS OF FORT MILES

As war clouds loomed in early 1940, the Harbor Defense of the Delaware (HDD) was created as one of 18 commands in the nation to guard the important ports. Each of the Harbor Defense commands was armed with many of the largest and most powerful weapons in the U.S. inventory.

It was the task of Fort Miles to protect the important port of Philadelphia with all of its vital industries. When Fort Miles was finally completed, it was one of the most heavily armed of all the HDD commands on the East Coast, with two 16-inch, two 12-inch, and four 6-inch guns. Only Fort Story, with four 16-inch guns, had more firepower. Ultimately, Fort Miles was to boast 12 batteries of weapons, including four major-caliber weapons that could reach targets from 17 to 25 miles off the coast.

In September 1940, army survey teams secretly started working along the coast in the Lewes area, identifying key sites for the fort. After negotiations with local and state officials for additional land not already owned by the federal government, work began on the fort in the spring of 1941. Ultimately the fort covered 1,300 acres along both the Delaware Bay and Atlantic Ocean. Construction was scheduled for the gun and mine batteries, the two largest being Battery Smith, the casemate for the two huge 16-inch guns, and Battery 519, the casemate for the two 12-inch guns that were to be moved from another Delaware World War I fort. Fortunately, this major effort was documented and is a part of this chapter.

In addition to the casemates, a series of 11 fire control towers would be built on the fort and to the south toward the Maryland line. Target-tracking and range-finding devices were located in the towers. These were the "eyes" of the fort and are today the most visible architectural landmarks along the Delaware Atlantic coastline.

A major job at the fort was tending the hundreds of mines that were to put in fields at the mouth of the Delaware Bay to stop both surface ships and later German submarines from entering the Delaware River. The placing, plotting, and tending of these mines involved hundreds of base personnel.

When finally completed, the fort had over 2,000 military and civilian personnel, including many women. It was one of the most secret places on the East Coast, and that is why so few photographs exist of wartime Fort Miles.

The first military unit sent to Fort Miles was the 261st Coast Artillery, a Delaware National Guard unit. This unit was to stay at the fort during almost all of the war and to this day is very proud of the fact that they were charged by the governor of Delaware to guard their homeland.

Notice the large truss for the casemate being elevated in the background during the construction of Battery Smith. The battery was the largest at Fort Miles and took the most effort to construct. Battery Smith was named in honor of Maj. Gen. William R. Smith. General Smith commanded the famous 36th Division of Texas during World War I, which won four citations.

Here is a close-up of casemate concrete forms and steel truss in the construction of Battery Smith. This battery was constructed between March 1941 and October 1942. The lumber forms give the interior concrete walls a finish that resembles wooden planks.

Here Casemate No. 2 at Battery Smith is being built on December 20, 1941, less than three weeks after Pearl Harbor. This casemate was built for two 16-inch MKII, Mod1 guns that, with tube and carriage, weighed over 500 tons. In the foreground, the circular gun pit is visible beneath the burster apron. The pit was more than 16 feet deep. It housed the mechanism that controlled the movement of the carriage.

The entrance to Battery Smith is built. There were three entrances to the battery, one in the middle for service and one each behind the two gun blocks. The letters on the top left of the door stand for United States Engineering Department.

In this picture of the front of Casemate No. 2 of Battery Smith, notice the concrete canopy constructed to burst incoming shells to keep them from penetrating the gun block.

Here is a close-up of the rear portal of Casemate No. 2 of Battery Smith. Supplies for the battery, including powder and shells for the huge guns, were moved through this entrance.

This is another long-distance photograph of the rear of Battery Smith's Casemate No. 2.

One of the huge 16-inch guns, the largest guns in the U.S. weapons inventory during World War II, arrives by train in June 1942. These built-up guns consisted of three main elements: the tube, the breech mechanism, and a liner that contained the rifling. The liners were removable. After 200 rounds, the gun began to lose accuracy due to damage caused by the heavy shells as they exited the guns, propelled by 900 pounds of explosives.

Here we see the cribbing and beams used in unloading the gun tubes from the railroad cars. The two 16-inch guns were made at the Watervliet, New York, and Midvale arsenals.

A truck and transporter start to move the gun tubes to Battery Smith from the railroad cars in July 1942.

Gun Tube No. 44 is shown on its way to the north casemate of Battery Smith. Notice the tremendous weight of the gun bearing down on the rear wheels of the transporter.

Gun Tube No. 110 is hauled to a temporary position at the entrance to the south casemate of Battery Smith in July 1942. When completed, this gun could fire shells over 25 miles at targets far over the horizon.

Here is another view of the cribbing and beams employed in positioning No. 110 in front of the south casemate. These guns were fired for the first time in February 1944.

Gun Tube No. 44 is shown in front of the entrance to the north casemate of Battery Smith. Each of the two gun blocks in the casemate was 43 feet by 43 feet. Today, one is the motor pool for the state park, the other is a gym!

This photograph shows the power ramming of a 16-inch casemated gun. Notice the size of the breech opening.

Here we see a 16-inch gun in front of a casemate. This is the final installed product, a fully functional 16-inch gun ready to shoot a 2,200-pound, armor-piercing shell at an enemy ship over 25 miles away. There are no extant photographs of the guns in place at Battery Smith; the appearance, however, would be very similar.

Storage was very important at Fort Miles. Near each battery were "igloos" that stored thousands of rounds of ammunition.

Each battery had enough shells to engage in a short combat, and when ammunition ran low, more supplies were brought to the batteries from these storage areas.

Battery Hunter was at the northern tip of the fort, a peer of Battery Herring with two 6-inch guns in shielded barbettes. Each gun fired a 105-pound shell a distance of over 14 miles.

This view of Battery Hunter is in the wintertime with snow on the battery. The shielded barbette protected the gun crew from counter fire. Note the earth-covered battery.

The second-largest casemated battery at Fort Miles was Battery 519, which had two 12-inch guns. This is a photograph of the completed southern casemate taken from the Fort Road in 1943.

Each of the Battery Herring and Battery Hunter guns sat on a ball-bearing turntable that allowed the guns to traverse 360 degrees.

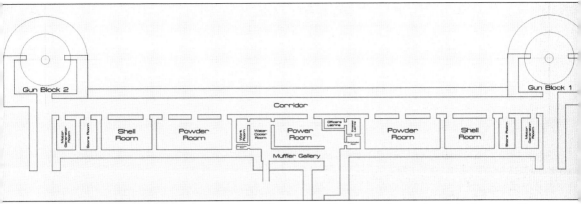

This drawing of Battery 519 shows the two 12-inch gun blocks at either end and the long corridor in between with powder and shell rooms. It is this battery that will be a World War II museum (chapter 5). Note that each gun operates individually, with separate powder, ammunition, and supplies. The confined space within the battery caused a number of unexpected problems. During the firing, the concussive blast of the gun caused the ventilation ducts to flatten out. Special reversing louvers had to be installed to prevent further damage. Cotton was provided for hearing protection, but it was not very effective.

The 12-inch gun fires its 970-pound, armor-piercing shell over 14 miles. It took 38 men in a gun section to operate the gun.

The front of the casemate of Battery 519 shows the steel gun-shield protecting the front of the gun. Sand was removed from the front of the gun and replaced by oiled rocks to hold down blast effects. This was one of two guns moved from nearby Fort Saulsbury.

One of the first units sent to Fort Miles was 8-inch railway (RY) guns from the 52nd Coast Artillery that practiced at Camp Henlopen during the prewar years. Here is the crew of Gun No. 1 on the 8-inch platform in May 1938.

During the firing of the 8-inch gun, notice the gun in recoil and the communications man to the left. There were to be eight 8-inch railway guns stationed at Fort Miles in two four-gun batteries—A and B. Each gun fired a 260-pound shell to a range of 17 miles.

This photograph shows the construction of an 8-inch railway revetment. Each revetment was constructed of concrete and sand bags covered with beach sand. The revetments were built between March and June 1942. Although they are currently covered with vegetation, the revetments can still be clearly seen.

REPORT OF COMPLETED WORKS – SEACOAST FORTIFICATIONS
(Battery Plan)

HARBOR DEFENSES OF THE DELAWARE
FORT MILES
BATTERY NO. 22
No. of Guns – 4   Caliber – 155   Carriage – Mobile

Part VII   Corrected to 1 JANUARY 1944

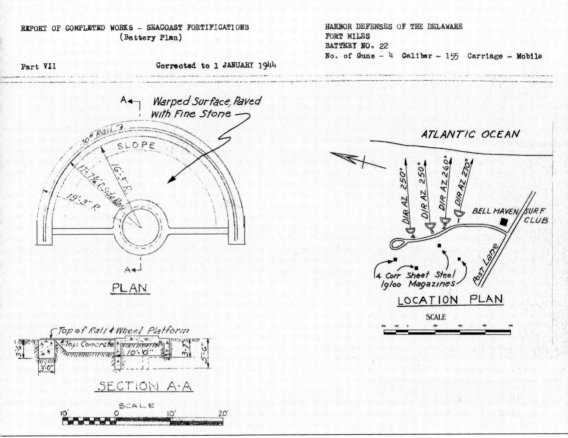

This map shows the position of both railway guns' spur track lines, ammunition igloos, and a "Panama mount" for one of the four 155-mm guns stationed at Fort Miles.

The first guns brought to Fort Miles were four 155-mm 1918 M1 mobile guns, the only mobile U.S. Army guns large enough for coast artillery. The four guns were ordered in April 1941 and sent to Camp Henlopen to be the first weapons installed on the beach in Battery 22. Each gun fired a 127-pound shell over 18 miles.

This is a photo showing a "Panama mount," first used at the Panama Canal to guard that vital area. The mount was 38 feet wide with a concrete platform in the middle to allow the gun to pivot. By placing the trail of the gun on the semi-circular arched rail, the gun could traverse 240 degrees. The park's bathhouse is built on this Panama mount.

Fort Miles had 11 of these U.S. Army fire control towers (FCT), positioned both in the fort and down the Delaware Atlantic coast to near the Maryland state line. Four towers were also across the bay at Cape May. They were the "eyes" of the fort, spotting the fall of shot of the long-range guns and sending that information back to the Fort Miles plot room to ready for the next "shoot." This tower is the tallest of the FCTs at 110 feet and is located within the fort reservation. It was one of the most important of the towers (tower importance can be measured by how many observation decks each had, from three to two to one), as its three observation slits were tied into the mine command of the fort as well as the long-range guns. It has a great view of both the harbor and the ocean and today is the only FCT that is open to the public.

This is Fire Control Tower 5 as it stands today. It was located several hundred yards from the water when constructed.

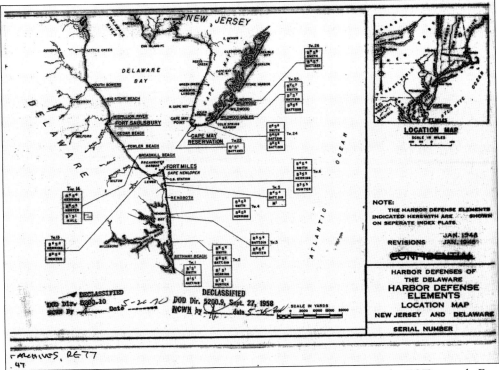

This unclassified map of the Delaware and New Jersey coastline shows the FCTs outside Fort Miles and the task of each of the observation decks of the towers in relation to the guns of the fort.

This is the construction of the 1,700-foot mine wharf. It was from this long pier that all ships arrived at the fort, including the German submarine U-858 in May 1945.

The mine wharf or pier was built to service the extensive mine fields of the fort. This was the largest job at the fort, taking much of the troops' time and effort. No matter what the weather conditions, the more than 400 mines in the bay had to be constantly serviced and maintained. Today this is a popular fishing pier at the Cape Henlopen State Park.

A close-up of the mine wharf and boat house shows where the fort's smaller boats that serviced the mines were docked. Notice the soldier walking his guard post on December 30, 1941.

Four

THE SURRENDER OF U-858
AT FORT MILES
May 14, 1945

When U-858 appeared off the Delaware coast on May 14, 1945, she was the first enemy warship to surrender to the United States since the War of 1812.

Fort Miles was built to combat the German surface fleet, but none ever appeared off the coast. Instead, what did appear was the German submarine force. Attacking the East Coast beginning in January 1942, German submarines destroyed hundreds of ships and killed thousands of sailors. The German Navy (*Kreigsmarine*) called this Operation Drumbeat. Many of the ships were destroyed within sight of the Delaware coast, so local citizens were witness to the desperate survival efforts of the stricken ships. The port of Lewes became a port of refuge for many sailors from the torpedoed ships.

The Germans continued to attack the East Coast throughout the war. Even in the spring of 1945, when the war was almost over, the *Kreigsmarine* had several attack boats off American shores. One of those boats was U-858, commanded by 27-year-old Kapitänleutnant Thilo Bode, with a crew of 57 officers and men. U-858 reached the Canadian shore, along with several other German submarines, in the spring of 1945. On May 4, 1945, the Kreigsmarine announced that hostilities were to stop on May 5. At that time Kapitänleutnant Bode found himself in Canadian waters. He decided to direct the boat to American waters and surrender. On May 9, she was ordered to surface, broadcast her position, run up either a white or black flag, and be prepared to surrender. Bode had his shower curtain painted black, surfaced the boat, and threw all the ammunition and even the barrels of the twin 20-mm cannons overboard so as to not appear threatening.

On May 10, 1945, off the coast of New Jersey, the submarine was located by U.S. Navy forces. Two ships (*Muir* and *Carter*) carefully approached the submarine in a fog bank, barely able to see the black flag. They then turned the submarine over to the destroyer escort (DE) *Pillsbury*. Along with the DE *Pope*, the *Pillsbury* placed a prize crew of Marines and Naval personnel aboard, searched the crew for documents and weapons, and took her official surrender at sea.

It was decided not to take the submarine to the nearest navy facility at Cape May as that harbor was too shallow. Rather, she was instructed to go to the deeper anchorage at Fort Miles.

The U.S. Marines and Navy personnel are in a whaleboat preparing their weapons to board U-858 and take the German sailors' surrender.

A whaleboat full of Marines and Navy personnel arrives at the bow of the submarine, and the prize crew is in the process of searching the German crewmen. German sailors were transferred to U.S. Navy ships and then to ships from Fort Miles.

U.S. sailors are above deck on a destroyer escort while German sailors below make ready to transfer to boats from Fort Miles.

The transfer at sea from U.S. Navy ships to those from Fort Miles is made. The German crew was then taken to the mine wharf at Fort Miles to be imprisoned by U.S. Army personnel.

A German sailor, probably Kapitänleutnant Bode, is shown jumping from a U.S. Navy ship to a boat from Fort Miles.

These German sailors are under guard on the fantail of a Fort Miles boat on their way to Fort Miles. Kapitänleutnant Bode is second from the left in back.

German sailors are enjoying American cigarettes on the boat to Fort Miles. Note the two submachine-gun-armed American guards, with the guard on the left pointing his weapon at the German crew.

This is a famous close-up photograph of Kapitänleutnant Bode smoking an American cigarette and glaring at the camera. Actually Bode was a rather jovial person who was happy to be alive in U.S. custody, as were his crewmen. He was only at Fort Miles one day and was then taken to Washington by Naval Intelligence to be questioned in detail about the capabilities of his boat. The United States was concerned that Germany had been able to link their V-1 and V-2 technologies with their deadly submarine force. After much probing, it was found that they had not been able to make the connection.

U-858 moves under its own power to Fort Miles. While most of the crew was transported to the fort by other vessels, the German engine room crew was tasked with bringing the boat safely to port under the watchful eye of the U.S. Navy officers on the conning tower. The German crew threw the twin 20-mm anti-aircraft guns overboard before they surrendered so as not the provoke the U.S. Navy.

U-858 approaches the Fort Miles mine wharf. Notice the white hats of U.S. Navy officers awaiting her arrival.

German crewmen disembark from a Fort Miles yawl to the mine wharf. On the wharf, they were lined up for their final search and surrender.

U-858 sailors are seen near the mine wharf in the stern of a yawl from Fort Miles. Note army trucks on the wharf ready to take the German crew to the brig at Fort Miles.

Kapitänleutnant Bode speaks to a U.S. Navy interpreter, Lt. Robert Braun, on the stern of a yawl nearing the mine wharf.

German crew in the stern of a Fort Miles yawl relax for the cameraman. Many of these captured German sailors did not get back to Germany until 1948.

The German crew stand at ease on the mine wharf at Fort Miles. Although most German sailors spoke some English, they would not acknowledge their American guards.

The other yawl from Fort Miles arrives with more German submariners ready to disembark at the mine wharf. The crew were to spend a few days at Fort Miles and were then transferred to Fort DuPont, the main German POW facility in Delaware.

Kapitänleutnant Bode arrives at the mine wharf with his back to the camera and his Red Cross survival pack under his arm. Note the armed American guards surrounding the crew.

Each crewman is again carefully searched. Here Kapitänleutnant Bode is undergoing his search.

Here documents are discovered on a U-858 sailor and removed. Note the American officers on the left checking the crew list.

Another German U-858 sailor is searched under the watchful eye of U.S. officers. Notice the truck in the background ready to take the sailors to the base brig.

Yet another crewman is searched while a helicopter hovers in the background watching the events.

A grim-faced, bearded German sailor is rather unhappy about being searched again. Notice his submariner waterproof pants.

After the search, an American officer informs the German crew what else is to take place in the surrender process. Note the rather dingy look of the German crew. The sub had been at sea since March 1945, and both the crew and the boat were dirty.

Kapitänleutnant Bode is reviewing documents with Comdr. J. P. Norfleet, U.S. Navy (retired), with Lt. Robert Braun interpreting.

German sailors boarded Fort Miles trucks to be taken to the brig, which was less than 1,000 yards away.

Here, the sailors arrive at the brig under the watchful eye of both the executive officer of U-858 and armed Fort Miles guards.

All German sailors' personal effects are carefully examined by Fort Miles staff.

A German sailor throws potato bags loaded with the personal effects and clothes of the submariners on a truck to be further examined by Fort Miles personnel.

The U-858 crew is lined up before leaving for mess, carefully guarded by Fort Miles soldiers.

German POWs get hot food under the watchful eye of Fort Miles staff. Notice most submarine sailors are still in their waterproof pants.

Five

An End and a New Beginning

At the conclusion of the war, Fort Miles was well into the process of standing down. The 16-inch and 12-inch batteries were deemed obsolete. The navy assumed command of the minefield and the six-inch batteries. Of course, the anti-aircraft units stayed on. The late 1940s saw the dismantling and disposal of the heavy guns. Fort Miles served as a training center for anti-aircraft troops going to Korea. The units fired their 90-mm guns at aircraft-towed targets or radio-controlled airplanes. The Separate Coast Artillery ceased to exist after the war.

In 1964, the army ceded a portion of Fort Miles to the State of Delaware. Cape Henlopen State Park was created on that land. Barracks, offices, mess halls, and other non-essential buildings were demolished or served as vacation apartments for the military. During the 1960s and 1970s, the navy converted Battery Herring into an underwater listening station. This super-secret installation used an array of microphones placed on the continental shelf to track Soviet submarines during the cold war. Thanks to the efforts of Sen. Joseph Biden, the balance of the land and remaining structures have been added to Cape Henlopen State Park.

Recently, the Division of Parks and Recreation has undertaken the task of creating a unique museum encompassing a portion of the old fort. Battery 519, the 12-inch battery, will serve as the indoor portion of the museum. The southern portion of the battery will retain its wartime appearance and feature a 12-inch gun donated by the navy.

The connecting hall between the gun rooms will feature exhibits that explore the war in the Atlantic as well as the Delaware home front. The north gun room will feature a modern recreation of the underwater listening station. Fifteen computer workstations provide visitors with an opportunity to listen to the sounds of the sea, both natural and man-made. Just inshore from the battery, a series of barracks and support buildings for the gunners is being restored. Planners envision an open-air living-history program in this setting.

The Fort Miles Historic Area provides a setting that will tell the stories of the veterans, the civilians, the construction workers, and the local residents who experienced the war where it touched the Delaware coast.

Standing Left to Right
Curtis A. Hausman
Earlen N. McCurry
Henry Yam
Ralph A.. Moses
Paul C. Jacobs
Robert T. Campbell
Jenmalhofer
Wingate
Rode

Seated Left to Right
Anthony J.Overmeyer
Stechel
Edward McDaniel
Ronald R. Merriman
Tagliaferri

FAREWELL BANQUET FOR
COAST ARTILLERYMEN
SERVING AT FORT MILES
DEL. 1942-1944. Held at
Sequoia Inn, Lewes, Del.
March 1944. 3 of 5 photos

Prior to war's end, the decreasing threat level at home allowed more coast artillery troops to be transferred to Europe, where their expertise was highly valued. Pictured here is a farewell party for parting friends.

A gleeful group of the first soldiers released from the army at the conclusion of the war come storming through the main gate at Fort Miles. This was just the first of many as the Separate Coast Artillery began to disband for the last time.

Gov. Walter Bacon reviews the troops at the conclusion of the war in this undated picture. At this time, Fort Miles was well on its way to obsolescence. The separate coast artillery itself was under review and would soon be disbanded. The rise and fall of this super seacoast fortification would span less than 10 years.

This is the new and very modern commissary. A wide variety of merchandise was available for the convenience of soldiers and their families on base. It was also something of a social hub with its snack-food restaurant.

Soldiers scramble to bring up another shell in this live fire exercise along the beach with 90-mm guns. Note the substantial supply of reloads under the tarp just behind the soldiers. The 90-mm maintained a very high rate of fire. Shells set with radio proximity fuses helped to insure the deadly accuracy of these weapons.

Anti-aircraft gunners fire at targets towed behind aircraft. Notice the telephone on the hip of the captain waving the flag.

Anti-aircraft training officers look over a 90-mm gun ready for target practice. The soldier seated on the right operates the position finder. This stereoscopic devise allows the sighter to track both the height and position of an aircraft.

The target's in sight! The battery sets up to begin its drill. Note the range-finding equipment behind the gun and the communication wire spread out over the sand.

This group of trainees is being instructed in the use and layout of tactical radios.

A technician works on an "R-Cat" or radio controlled air target. The R-Cats took the place of pilot-towed targets after the gunners began to become just a bit too proficient for comfort. Removing the chance for disaster, gunnery practice became more realistic as the experienced R-Cat flyers dipped and turned their aircraft, simulating actual combat in a much more realistic fashion.

Soldiers load the ammunition clip into this rapid-fire anti-aircraft piece as officers look on.

Training in anti-aircraft artillery was not the only activity at Fort Miles in the postwar years. Here a soldier gets tips on cover and concealment.

Fire Control Tower 6 is seen here with the remnants of its generator building. Again note the position of the tower far from the ocean.

This is Col. Riley McGarraugh, the last commanding officer at Fort Miles. Colonel McGarraugh served in both world wars and the Korean War. During World War II, the colonel was commander of the anti-aircraft artillery defenses at Oran, Africa, and then head of the Joint Artillery Infantry Board at Fort Benning, Georgia. McGarraugh served on General McArthur's staff in the Far East, receiving a Legion of Merit Award. He assumed command of Fort Miles in 1952, retiring in 1954 after receiving the Conspicuous Service Cross of the State of Delaware.

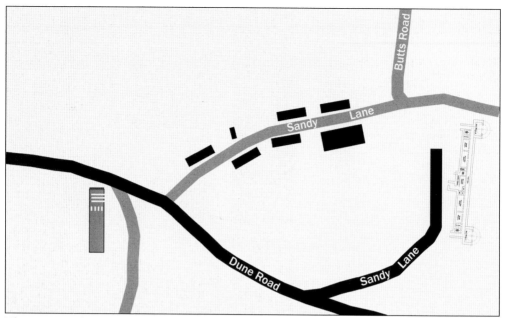

This map of the Fort Miles Historic Area shows the buildings that will comprise the new outdoor museum. The buildings along Sandy Lane were home to the gunners at Battery 519. They include a recreation building, a supply and administration building, four barracks, and a modern orientation building. The gun battery housing the main museum is underground at the left of the page. Fire Control Tower 7 is open to the public, providing a spectacular view of the ocean and bay.

A 3-inch gun arrives at the gun park. Located among the barracks on Sandy Lane are a number of guns representing the various types found at Fort Miles during the war. In this picture, Delaware National Guardsmen deliver the 3-inch, .50-caliber gun to the site after its trip from Fort Howard near Baltimore.

This 6-inch gun is on loan from the U.S. Navy. This gun was found in excellent condition at the Naval Surface Warfare Center in Dahlgren, Virginia. Here the gun is shown slipping into the key way on the mount. While the operation may look simple enough, the work actually took more than two weeks. Gun and mount had been living separately for more than 30 years and required some reacquainting.

The finished product, the 6-inch gun sits on its mount surrounded by a sandbag revetment. Visitors delight in elevating and traversing the gun. The 8-inch gun can be seen in the foreground.

A one-of-a-kind 8-inch gun is delivered to its pad by crane. The gun was built by the army for the navy, who never used it. In this photograph, the gun is being lowered onto its carriage. This gun had not been separated from its mount in more than 65 years. Safe travel required the separation of the two.

Seabees work to properly replace the tube on the carriage. Working with one-of-a-kind brass fittings required skill and care, which were provided by this volunteer team.

The 8-inch gun is shown after being restored and sports a gleaming new coat of paint. The gun will be mounted on a railroad flatbed car as soon as a suitable one is located, enabling staff to better interpret the role of the railroad guns of Fort Miles.

The 18812, a MK 7, 12-inch, .50-caliber gun weighing in at an impressive 90 tons, awaits preservation prior to being moved into Battery 519. This gun was manufactured for and mounted on the Battleship *Wyoming*. A navy master chief described it as rusty but regal. The gun mount is visible beneath the trees.

After an "extreme makeover," the tube is ready for the next step, moving inside the gun battery and being mounting on its carriage.

The *Wyoming* was laid down at the William Cramp and Sons shipyard in Philadelphia on February 9, 1910, and was commissioned at the Philadelphia Naval Yard on September 25, 1912. She was one of the most powerful ships in the world at the time, being armed with twelve 12-inch, .50-caliber MK 7 guns in six two-gun turrets. She displaced over 27,000 tons and was 562 feet long. She participated in World War I as part of Battleship Division 9 which included the *Delaware* (BB-28). The *Wyoming* was one of the navy ships that escorted the German High Seas Fleet to the Firth of Forth on November 21, 1918. After the war, she was converted to a gun-training ship as per the terms of the London Treaty in 1930, and several of her powerful 12-inch turrets were removed. Working out of the Chesapeake Bay for much of the remainder of her career, she was nicknamed by sailors the "Chesapeake Raider" for all the time she spent in that area training gun crews. When World War II began, the remainder of her 12-inch guns were removed and she trained over 35,000 gunners on seven types of anti-aircraft weapons, which became very important in the Pacific War against the new Japanese kamikazes. After the war, she was decommissioned on August 1, 1947, and the ship was scrapped in Kearney, New Jersey in 1947–1948.

Fort Miles was named after the great American hero Nelson Appleton Miles (1839–1925) in 1941, though many Delawareans would have preferred to have the fort named after a local hero. On August 5, 1941, by order of the secretary of war, Camp Henlopen's name was officially changed to Fort Miles. This order was released to the press on August 11, 1941, and the reason why the fort was named as it was became clear in the order, as the son of Gen. Nelson Miles was Brig. Gen. Sherman Miles, Assistant Army Chief of Staff, G-2. Nelson Miles was born in Westminster, Massachusetts, on August 8, 1839. At the beginning of the Civil War, he impressed all those who served with him. He became a major general barely two months after his 26th birthday. After a rapid promotion, he became a corps commander at the end of the war. He was sent out West after the Civil War to help tame the American Indian rebellion. Miles also was the commander who finally closed the frontier by ending the American Indian uprising in 1890. Later, in the Spanish-American War, he commanded the force that captured Puerto Rico. He was named commander in chief of the U.S. Army in October 1895 and held that title until August 1903. He was the last commander in chief of the army, as after his death, the title was changed to chief of staff.

BIBLIOGRAPHY

Grayson, William C. *Delaware Ghost Towers*. Bloomington, IN: Authorhouse Press, 2005.

Hogg, Ian V. *The American Arsenal*. London: Greenhill, 2001.

Jennings, Lee. *Fort Miles Past and Future*. Dover, DE: 2002.

Kaufmann, J. E., and H. W. Kaufmann. *Fortress America*. Cambridge, MA: Perseus Books, 2004.

Lewis, E. R. *Seacoast Fortifications of the United States*. Annapolis, MD: Naval Institute Press, 1970.

Miller, David. *U-Boats*. Dulles, VA: Pegasus Press, 2005.

Photographs of Fort Miles. RG 1325.003.206, Box 6, Delaware Public Archives, Dover.

———. Wesley Banase Collection. Personal Photographs.

———. Horace Knowles Collection. Personal Photographs.

———. Fred Ruleman Collection. Personal Photographs.

———. Will Smith Collection. Personal Photographs.

Photographs of the Fort Miles Players. Bill Frank Collection. Historical Society of Delaware, Wilmington.

"Records of the Corps of Engineers Philadelphia District 1941–1944." RG 77, Box 4, NARA, Branch Depository, Philadelphia.

"Records of the United States Army, Coastal Artillery Districts and Defenses, 1901–1942." RG 392, Box 570724, NARA, Silver Spring, MD.

"Records of the United States Army Commands—1942—Fort Miles." RG 330, Boxes 959/960. NARA, Silver Spring, MD.

Wasch, Diane Shaw, and Perry Bush. Arlene R. Kriv, ed. *World War II and the U.S. Army Mobilization Program: A History of 700 and 800 Series Cantonment Construction*. Washington, D.C.: U.S. Department of Defense.